Bathroom PRISONERS

Laura Lewis-Waters

Bent Key Publishing

First published in Great Britain by Bent Key Publishing, 2022
Copyright © Laura Lewis-Waters, 2022
The moral right of the author has been asserted.

All rights reserved. No part of this book may be reproduced in any form or by any electronic or mechanical means, including information storage and retrieval systems, without permission in writing from the publisher, except by reviewers, who may quote brief passages in a review.

ISBN: 978-1-915320-05-6

Bent Key Publishing
Owley Wood Road, Weaverham
bentkeypublishing.co.uk

Edited by Rebecca Kenny @ Bent Key
Cover art © Samantha Sanderson-Marshall @ Smash Design and Illustration
smashdesigns.co.uk

Printed in the UK by Mixam UK Ltd.

For Shaun

Contents

Preface 7

Steps to conceive with OCD: 9

You 11

Me 25

Us 45

Acknowledgements / About the author 55

About Bent Key 59

Previous publications 60

Preface

It was 2020. Like everyone else I found myself suddenly confined to my house. I'd recently found out that I was pregnant after years of trying and suffering a loss, and I was terrified and alone. At the time nobody knew the effects of COVID in pregnancy and my husband, who has suffered with OCD for some years now, and in his best efforts to keep me safe and well, caused further anxiety asking that we take extra precautions and stay completely inside as much as possible.

Bathroom Prisoners is about a vicious cycle of my husband's OCD affecting my own mental health, which in turn, affected us both. Everything was amplified due to being trapped at home together during lockdown. The poems explore the effects of anxiety on both ourselves as well as those around us. They are learning to deal with someone else's anxiety before realising they have their own to come to terms with. They also evoke a sense of place (home) due to the nature of lockdown. Sometimes they are the quiet moments sitting down with a cup of tea and sometimes they scream at the walls.

On, off, on, off, on, off, on...

Steps to conceive with OCD:

1. Tap toothbrush, tap light switch, tap foot, tap pedal, tap head
2. Wipe the bits off your feet when you get into bed
3. Make sure lids are screwed on just right
4. Read words out loud; through gritted teeth; don't read
5. Bury pants at the bottom of the drawer because they have red fluff on them; pretend blood does not exist
6. Don't make eye contact with the bathroom drawer, the one with all the tests; blink quickly to erase the image
7. Don't admit anything out loud

wonder why it still didn't work.

YOU

Case Study: Background Information

Examine your prison, every now and again,
focus. Do it slowly. With regard.
Your hands are wet. Make a mental note
where: bathroom
            first home
                     end terrace
when: 13 times a day
            (the house number)
                          (your birthday)
      (unlucky.)
how: a switch in your head
                (is this the same for all inmates?)

how's the weather: frosted glass grey
                        damp greenery
      mould.

What else do you notice? Anything of interest?
Focus. Do it slowly. With resolve.
You are alive. Make a mental note

Bathroom Prisoners (I)

Within four white walls
and a narrow window
you become a slave to the soap
scrubbing another layer of raw reddened skin
a mountain of sodden flannels
slowly rising to pay homage –
ritualistic bleeding creates micro cuts that
open up on your hands making you more
susceptible.

But captive behind steamed PVC, the
contaminated outside remains obscured
you exfoliate with sandpaper and renewed fear
even when the quarantine(d) captives are set free
you'll still be here in isolation, a
prisoner of the bathroom.

You shuffled into the room
hands out, palms up in front
in your head the blood bottled
and brimmed and trickled tenderly
onto the carpet we had once lovingly picked out
the stain penetrating and saturating
alongside the dread that pumped
through your veins.

Tiny shards of glass cling to your blue shirt
like impossible fragments of ice, already
infiltrating your skin through the holes in your clothes
and your face, through your mouth
blood bile rising.

For the rest of the day you bite down hard
the metallic swell ebbing through your nerve walls
puncturing and perforating your organs until
your eyes begin to drip as you look to me for
reassurance.

I smile at the broken glass in the sink
the one decorated with baubles from
a happy Christmas past.

I'm not
the hand washing
arm washing
face washing
eye washing
nasal spraying
hand washing
body washing
neck washing
leg washing
nasal spraying
hand creaming
mask wearing
breath holding
face peeling
hand scrubbing
skin blistering
food quarantining
wide awaking
one,
because ASDA brought a food delivery to the door.

There Is Safety in Monotony

breakfast dog outside panic
wash lunch cat inside panic
wash dinner me meat panic
wash breakfast dog outside
panic wash lunch cat inside
panic wash dinner me meat
panic wash breakfast dog
outside panic wash lunch cat
inside panic wash dinner me
meat panic wash breakfast
dog outside panic wash lunch
cat inside panic wash dinner
me meat panic wash panic

Match up the following:

You		due to
	mow the lawn	
1. forgot to	take the bin out	a) laziness
	pick your clothes up	
2. couldn't	brush your teeth	b) fear
	go for a walk	
3. refused to	you weren't alone	c) doubt
	not wash your face	
4. wouldn't	take the cups to the sink	d) hassle

I dance around the margins of pages ready to stop you from falling off, equally ready to pull you back up. Your doubts always between the lines I stumble over, each unsaid word a hurdle I'm not always tall enough to jump. Your chest is two neatly punched holes, rabbit holes, and I'm terrified you'll lose your footing and fall through whilst I remain on the other side of that warning red cordon. And in the blank spaces your own lines become inexact, inaudible, until I learn how to lip read.

A Drive to the Supermarket

I didn't hit anything, did I?
That bike was far enough away, wasn't it?
There was nothing behind, was there?
The pedestrian had enough room, didn't they?
The light wasn't red, was it?

You skip out in excitement for
the reduced section, your hobby,
but tonight you will have waking dreams of
red lights and splayed bodies.

vicious

circle (reading clockwise from top): mind letter paper cut words wash wife walls cat dog thoughts virus hands people attack bicycle bleach door handles

Radiation

Now it was your turn
to stand before me

witness for yourself
reactor meltdown

all because the sky
was grey, the temperature

13 degrees. Making
my core unstable

I had nothing to wear
you wouldn't dress me.

And then you did it.

You turned your back.

You thought I didn't see
the shake of your head

hear the subtle sigh
as you wash your hands.

You became the digits
in my watch, rising

laughing as my head
collided with my hand.

You watched as I destroyed
myself from the inside

when all I wanted
was the stability

your control rod arms.

And then you walked away.

ME

Bathroom Prisoners (II)

Life has come to exist at bathroom door boundaries, me,
involuntarily suspended on thresholds by the bathroom prisoner.

I suppose I was like a prison guard, always watching, but,
I was also a prisoner myself, except I had one foot in and one out.

In sanitary rooms, by which I mean any room with a sink,
towels hang limp, drenched with dread.

I survey the suspect with tenderness and terror, he,
works the same bacterial stain over and over, punishment.

Living with a prisoner confined me in other ways too:
a support mechanism, a voice of reassurance

yes, your hands are clean now
no, you didn't forget to clean the switch before turning on the water

But boundaries are small places and it would be possible to
suffocate in steam,
it would be possible to disappear.

Medical History

Patient: Laura Lewis-Waters   *Age: 30*

I have been pregnant, twice. Carried two, given birth to one. When my son was born, I nearly died. If I can tap my toothbrush just right, I'll admit to having O – C – D. I like to think I caught it from my husband who has Talipes and anxiety. There's always a Sertraline strip on the windowsill. My mother has, and my mother's father had, diabetes. She shares a B12 deficiency with my sister. My other sister has coeliac. My brother is too scared to know his own diagnosis. I don't drink. Don't smoke. I worry. Thyroxine for living. Clomid for hope. My grandmother died of a heart attack. My grandfather disappeared. Great Grandad lost a finger. Uncle Fred died aged 3. And, as I understand it, there can be life after death.

Adverse Effects

I've begun to get sweaty palms
in that very last moment
just before they announce
which design they will choose
on Garden Rescue

but,
I'm not even interested
in gardening
I think

Living with someone else's anxiety

is adopting it as your own
it's realising you have counted
black linoleum squares 1000 times
sat on the bathroom floor incapable
of standing up.

It is learning magic tricks the way you learnt
to ride a bike, slowly, painfully,
rituals that have to be adhered to
a couple a day at first until every little task
that keeps you alive is riddled with them –
it's turning the tap on off on off just because
you brushed your teeth
and always stepping into a room with your right foot
because if you don't you'll never conceive.

It's being your own failure
you feel selfish for acknowledging
because you are the 'normal' one, the unmedicated one,
reassurance that asbestos is not in the
crumbling Artex one.

It is filling in the gaps in the grout
so one day the house can be sold as a show home
when all you really want is to fall down
those little hollows.

It is slamming doors, crying,
collecting swimming certificates faster than anyone
around you, legs growing tired, throbbing
beneath the water.

It is befriending magnolia walls because
your husband, best friend, sister, colleague
are the ones that need you.

"I fucking hate living here"

I scream it at the top of my voice letting the words skim and saturate the air and hope, no pray, that they cut your skin and enter your body so that you too can be wounded.

But of course you are already wounded and the tears slip as the door shakes and rumbles inside me an earthquake that I must swallow back down to its epicentre in my core. But my voice still shakes and cracks appear in my tone, between my teeth, cavities widening that I must bridge and cross before it is too late.

"I'm sorry,"

I whisper, as I cradle my slightly swollen belly, hoping that my apology will linger in the air for long enough.

The I in Pity

I sometimes ask myself
if I'd have known
that one day I would
learn to pity
myself, would I have
made the same choices

- yes, I would.

The I in Selfish

I read once
there is a fine line
between

selfish & ―――――
――――― selfless

how can I ever
be the one he needs

if I only ever exist
on the left of that line?

Voice of Reassurance

At 7.17 you roll over
trying to keep your bleary
eyes open long enough
to ask me the time.

It's 20 past, I tell you
praying that you will not
reach over to check
for yourself.

Someone

Have you ever looked at someone
and for a fleeting second
forgotten who they are
how it was, that you'd
allowed this person to
lie next to you for the
past nine years
a stranger's eyes looking
quizzically back at you
with the power to haunt
you for hours after?

There Is No Safety in Monotony

There are only so
many times
he can ask

that was okay wasn't it

before I begin
to ask myself.

Ritual Magic

In the mornings I drink tea
from a mug with my name on it
to remind myself of who I am,

in the afternoon I drink
from a plain mug
to forget.

Ritualistic Tapping

until death d we part/ dis rder/ y ur bad behavi ur/ and y ur unpleasant th ughts/ where did y u even c me fr m/ my t thbrush is clean/ n ff/ n ff/ ST P/ there is n s ap/ can I leave the h use n w/ please st p/ c ndition/ d ct r?

when an we part/ ompulsion/ where did you even ome from/ an you stop/ he k/ he k/ he king I'm sane/ mental onditioning/ am I the ondition/ please lose/ I'm lean/ lean/ the toothbrush is lean/ do tor don't _ _

until eath o we part/ isease/ your ba attitu e/ nee s a can o attitu e/ where i you even come from/ unwante thoughts/ and tap tap tapping repeate ly/ I can o better/ my han s are clean/ octor on't refer me

39

Ritualistic Reading

It started with words in books
I started tapping them out on
my skin but even that is marked
with scars and moles that tell
stories of their own.

It spread to social media and
the news so that I couldn't
even be a part of
what was going on in the
world anymore.

It spread to my own words
so that I could not even
scribble incoherently
to myself at 4 am without
heart rate rising.

Sometimes I grind my teeth together
drawing the letters in my
mouth, hoping this way
I am able to read
more than a page in 15 minutes.

I tri ed rea ding alou d
en un ci a ting every las t lett
er, especially ts and ds
which I foun d par tic u lar ly
diff i cult to overcome.

I even tried to s l o w   d o w   n
enough to spit out

O	C	D

so I could read my own
diagnosis

                into being.

The Deflation of Words

I feel more positive than I have in a long time. I heard the neighbour on the other side of the fence; as soon as the words became buoyant on warm air I thought about the washing up, the cat sick by the bed, the germs outside the gate, the amount of times I would have to tap my toothbrush today before my mind told me I'd done it just right.

Bet you didn't know toothbrushes are fate determiners. Or that not cleaning them correctly can lead to miscarriage.

Before the words had been spoken I'd felt pretty positive myself. But I would have never acknowledged it.

Lugubrious

It had sat there all day
the notification
on my phone
sandwiched between *can't sync data* and *software update*

word of the day:

loo-goo-bree-uhs

just like the radio I slid
from mournful to downright
dismal. At just a word
I had turned myself into
a petulant child
a tantruming teenager
a pathetic woman
with no space for happiness,
or change, just like my phone.

A Story of Thieves and Witches

A thief, you stole into my life
when I wasn't looking. Slowly,
with certainty, taking everything
until you'd stolen my every
last thought. And when I had
nothing, I began to practise witchcraft;
rituals and incantations
to burn you. But my witchfire
was fuel and you became angrier
I performed more magic, more fire,
applied my potions slowly, with certainty
watched on helpless as you
stole my happiness, my peace, my time.

US

Shadows

We have become shadows in our home
pale imitations of ourselves that float
around hoping to be transparent
because that would mean we wouldn't have to
touch anything solid.
Contaminated.
We are both shadows
and would be scared of our shadows
if we had them.
We've forgotten the warmth of sunlight
sweet fresh air.
Our house is darkness, afraid even
of the windows.

But even shadows need light
to survive.

We keep a distance
even from each other,
but occasionally we gravitate towards
each other with an old love
until we merge
and blister.

We sit staring at the same nonsense on tv
the same water mark flowering
like a blood stain on the ceiling
the same scar on the wall from when
my phone hand got angry.
There is some talk
sometimes it is lifeless
words leak out of us
to fill gaps, cross roads
sometimes it is discoloured with words
to address what is going on in your head.
We pick at each other's scabs until
we are both pockmarked from a thousand battles –
you want me to be open, understanding
I want you to heal quicker
as if scratching at surface wounds
would ever allow for that.
Sometimes there is laughter
you can't go upstairs because
a pair of contaminated jeans has fallen from the banister
we laugh together,
sometimes I laugh alone, it's either that
or something worse
like when you stood at the backdoor frozen
in horror as a beach ball came over the fence.
I laugh because I hope
laughter can stitch together our laceration
the way it does after a regular argument
when we decide we can't be bothered to fight
anymore and a slight smirk turns into
hysterics at the ridiculousness.

I laugh to fill the silent spaces, the
crevasses that lead from one stress to the next.
I laugh because I hope you'll hear me
on the occasions when our home spans different postcodes,
and I laugh because I hope you'll laugh with me
and everyone else will laugh with us

The walls look tired.

I thought the cracks were created
by nearby trains that shake the house,

but I have started to wonder if instead they are
tired of listening to our issues and anxieties, each

whispered doubt working its way deeper into the plasterboard
scarring the magnolia.

But what if we could

fill those channels with understanding
and love, piece by piece dredging out the fears

of something worse living in there
until the walls are no longer run-down

Why is it that we can't keep a plant alive in this house?

Is the environment so toxic
that even those
that need such little care
can not keep
their little heads up
and those
who just ask
for a little light
can see not even a pinprick
and those
who thought they had
an ability to thrive
in the darkest conditions
continue to wilt

- *is it that we just can't be bothered?*

We

used to be linked by the collective pronoun
we were one/ in sync/ in unison
we travelled all the way to Iceland to figure out that we,
we could become a we and not two I's
wandering around bumping into others.
We travelled back again to a church
with peeling white paint and defied the two tectonic plates that had
separated in the distance
to become a we written on paper so that we could
file us in the important paper box on the shelf in the wardrobe
official.

We were always a good match:
you liked the sponge, I liked the icing
you liked numbers, I preferred words
opposites in many ways but equal in hopes,
we would overcome anything.

But when did there become a you and I/me and you/him and her?

Was it when you started lying awake at night
without me, jumping more fences than those sheep would ever know?
Or
when you began to shoulder burdens that I could not understand?

Or perhaps you had to grieve alone when I
was too selfish to see anything beyond my own emptiness?
Back in Iceland we were only kids really.
We may have been young, lacking the
foresight to see our faults. But they are
OUR faults and we will overcome them
together. As a we. As an us.

Home

We bought a house today

the paint is peeling
the wiring is old
it smells of damp

we'll make it our new family home, we thought.

Suddenly the sun
crested on the clouds
and we completely
forgot about the storms
that had wracked and ruined
our ship for so long.

Acknowledgements

Firstly, I would like to thank Rebecca — without her this book would not exist. Thank you for seeing something within these pages and for making dreams come true. Thank you to my supervisors at Loughborough, Jennifer Cooke and Kerry Featherstone, for the feedback and for making me feel capable. Also to Katharine Perry, The Mum Poem Press and The Mum Poet Club Members for all of the support and confidence you have given me. You have really helped me to start writing again.

And, of course, thank you as always to my family. Thank you for always listening to my writing and for the encouragement. Shaun — my endless gratitude for everything. This would not exist without you. Thank you for allowing me to be so open and honest.

About the Author

Laura Lewis-Waters is a poet, English teacher and research student from the Midlands, where she lives with her husband and son. She is currently working towards her PhD at Loughborough University writing poetry about sea level rise. More recently, she has begun writing about teaching, motherhood and mental health as a result of lockdown.

Her poems have appeared in Streetcake Experimental Writing Magazine, Public Sector Poetry Journal, and The Mechanics Institute Review; she was longlisted for the Streetcake Experimental Writing Prize in 2020. In 2013, she worked briefly as a journalist for a prominent newspaper in Singapore.

Instagram: @lauralewis_waters

About Bent Key

It started with a key.

Bent Key is named after the bent front-door key that Rebecca Kenny found in her pocket after arriving home from hospital following her car crash. It is a symbol - of change, new starts, risk and taking a chance on the unknown.

Bent Key is a micropublisher with ethics. We do not charge for submissions, we do not charge to publish and we make space for writers who may struggle to access traditional publishing houses, specifically writers who are neuro-divergent or otherwise marginalised. We never ask anyone to write for free, and we like to champion authentic voices.

All of our beautiful covers are designed by our graphic designer Sam at SMASH Illustration, a graphic design company based in Southport, Merseyside.

Find us online:
bentkeypublishing.co.uk

Instagram/Facebook   @bentkeypublishing
Twitter   @bentkeypublish

Previous Publications

Vicious featured in Streetcake Experimental Writing Magazine, Issue 77, March 2022

Case Study: Background Information longlisted for the Streetcake Experimental Writing Prize 2020